Is She The ONE?

LaKesha Womack

ISBN: 9781442199132

This book is dedicated

to my son,

Kristian Womack.

I hope that you live

to laugh and love

with a lifelong mate.

This book is written for the man who thinks he has found the right woman and is ready to make the ultimate commitment - marriage. Granted, I am not a man, but I am a woman who has seen plenty of her guy friends walk through the decision-making process to get married, counseled them through staying married and supported them when things didn't work out.

Like most events in life, I've lost some and won some. Although they weren't my battles to fight, I found it difficult to see my friends going through these trials and tribulations in their relationships. This book is filled with my opinions based on the experiences that I have been a part of and my desire to encourage relationships built on a strong foundation of love, communication and understanding. I hope that reading this will provide you with some insight into figuring out if she is the ONE so that when you say, "I do" it will be forever.

It is my belief that some men get married when they reach a certain point in their life. You may have a job that pays a decent wage, you feel like you can financially take care of a family, or you find a girl so far out of your league that you think the only way to keep her is to pop the question (I know that most guys won't 'fess up to this one, but it's ok). In these situations, there are no fireworks, no cosmic alignment of the stars, no overwhelming sense that your life is incomplete without her; you are just ready to take the next step in your life – starting a family. If you find yourself in one of these situations, it is very necessary for you to create some parameters to judge whether the woman standing before you is the one you can spend the rest of your life with.

I will concede... there are some men out there that fall madly in love with a woman. So much so that they love everything about her from her split ends to her ingrown toenails. This is the ideal scenario and one that we should all strive for. After all, who is not seeking unconditional love? However, you have to be sure that the whirlwind of emotions that sometimes embody falling in love involves some rational thinking. Marriage is a lifelong commitment. It should not be something that is here today and gone tomorrow.

Getting married and staying married is a choice. It is a choice that you have to remind yourself, possibly on a daily basis that you willingly undertook. Throughout your journey together, you will be faced with many temptations. You may meet someone who is more attractive, that you perceive to be better in bed or that stimulates you more intellectually. It is during these times that you have to reflect on all of the things about your wife that made you decide that she is the ONE.

I believe the divorce rate is so high in our society because we are no longer getting married for the right reasons. Not only have many people given up on love but some aren't even being practical about their decisions. You want someone that you can live with without wanting to kill – everyday; while she wants a younger, sexier version of her father. There is a chance that both of you will end up with the perfect mate and a lifelong union, but the majority of relationships end in divorce with hopes of become wiser the next time around.

If you want to get it right this time, get in gear for these ten projects and learn some things about your woman that will serve as a crystal ball into some of her tendencies. Notice that I said tendencies because people are unpredictable, but we are going to focus on increasing your probability of a successful partnership. There will still be things about her that it will take years to figure out, but you should have a clearer view about some important aspects of her personality and decision-making process, which will in turn help you to better communicate with her.

Some people may think these projects are tricky or a way of being underhanded, but I don't see it that way. I think every situation can be viewed positively or negatively. I prefer to see these projects from a positive perspective. It is hard to really get to know people because they have become very good at introducing you their representatives, the person that they want you to know or the person that they want to be. Sometimes, you are falling in love with her representative and feel like you get your formal introduction to your lifelong mate once you put a ring on it. These projects are a way for you to see beyond what is immediately being presented to you and attempt to gain a deeper understanding of the person you are planning to commit the rest of your life to.

I've heard so many people, not just men; say that their mate changed once they got married. It could be true, but I find it hard to believe that they completely changed. I think that sometimes there wasn't enough due diligence done on the front end because the couple felt it was time to take the plunge, for whatever reason. My motto is: what does it matter if we wait a few months if we are planning to spend the rest of our lives together. If either of you are rushing to get marriage, that should be a red flag because an eternal bond can begin without a ceremony. That's not an endorsement for keeping her on the hook for an extended period. I'm just saying take some time to get to know her. If you have been in a relationship with a woman for more than three years and you are still not sure whether you want to marry, I have another book for you...

I wish you the best of luck and hope to receive many wedding invitations and many more letters of gratitude years from now.

At the end of each section, you can make a decision. Did she come across as a gold digger (all about your dividends), a drama queen (nothing but theatrics) or The ONE (just as you expected or possibly exceeding your expectations)? Some of the descriptions may not fit the situation perfectly but you're a smart guy, you can judge which area she fits most closely.

By the way, I don't think it's a problem if you like drama queens or gold diggers but it's only fair that you recognize this before you pop the question. Otherwise, you may wake up one day wondering why you're broke or why she's always stressing you out. These titles are only meant as a generalization and should not be taken to mean your girl has an inherent character flaw or that you should be running for the hills.

I have some girlfriends that are drama queens and some that are gold diggers and their men worship the ground they walk on. They do so because they accept the women for who they are and choose to focus on their goodness and not the other stuff.

We all have the desire to be loved unconditionally. I pray for you to love her with all of your heart and without any hesitation or reservation and that she loves you the same.

Letter to the ladies:

Some of you may not understand why I decided to write this book, but I hope most of you will appreciate my good intentions. It is my desire to make the matrimonial union stronger by encouraging men, as well as women, to get to know their mates on a deeper level prior to making a lifelong commitment.

If you found this book in your man's possession, don't get mad. First, you should be happy that he is considering popping the question (Congratulations!), then happy that he is taking the time to be sure of his decision and that he seems to have a sincere desire to better understand who you are as a person.

If you bought this book to see what all of the hype is about, I hope you enjoy it and share it with your girlfriends. Put yourself in a couple of these scenarios to see how you would really react. Don't use it as a weapon to try to trick him into thinking that you are "The ONE" because the joke could be on you in the end if he finds out that you are not who you presented yourself to be. I am not an advocate for divorce, but relationships are much like business contracts. You each have a responsibility to be honest and truthful to one another, if one party defaults on the contract, is it fair to hold the other person accountable to keeping their end of the deal?

My relationship philosophy is to find out all of the good **and** the bad stuff upfront because we are all human. We all have flaws but before I hitch my horse to your cart, I need to know that we are planning to travel in the same direction. I don't want a man that doesn't have the desire to get to know me on a deeper level. If he is just about my looks or getting my goodies then he can keep it moving. I may not always be this cute and we all know what they say about sex once you get married so I need to know that when we are 80 years old, our relationship will still have some substance.

Grab your favorite drink and enjoy!

What is _my_ definition of true love?

True love is seeing the absolute worst characteristics of a person or being around them when you feel like you just can't take it anymore and realizing that you would rather be with them than without them.

Is She The ONE?

One

Family First

Many guys make the mistake of only visiting their girl's family during a holiday. Big mistake! Although they may or may not be your favorite people, you all are about to become one big happy family. Everyone knows that the holidays are a time for food, festivities, fussin' and frontin.' We are putting on airs, pulling out the good dishes, flossing for family members that we rarely see and doing all that we can to show that our lives are perfect.

I love being around my family during the holidays, not only because I love to eat, but because it is great to see everyone in such a festive environment. Visiting during non-holidays can sometimes be a different story. I'm sure you've been to visit a relative just because you were in town and everything was cool, but it just wasn't as.... festive. There aren't as many people around to mingle with, so you have to have real conversations and they start asking questions. Questions that you don't always want to answer. Then they start telling stories. Stories you are sure you have heard a million times and probably don't ever want to hear again.

Where am I going with this? You all need to visit each other's family during a non-holiday period.

Your objective is to get a good glimpse of her relationship with her family. You never know where you are going until you know where you came from. You also need to see how she is going to get along with your family. During the holidays it may be easy for her to avoid talking to your mother because everyone is so busy hustling and bustling around but during a calm family weekend your mother and other family members will have a chance to really get to know the person that is about to join their family. It will be important for her family to have the same opportunity with you.

Tony and Sheila were dating for two years. Tony always dreaded going to visit Sheila's parents because he had better things to do – or so he thought. I would ask him about her family and he just responded, "They're a'ight." I expected more information or more of a reaction but never got one. It wasn't until they started planning their wedding that he realized what he was dealing with. Her mom and sisters were so controlling of every decision that he felt like he no longer had a voice in his own wedding.

Tony thought that this would pass once the wedding was over. WRONG ANSWER!! It actually got worse. Sheila's sisters and mom were so involved in every aspect of his relationship that he would often complain that he felt like he had four wives instead of one.

This is partly true because Tony never took the time to figure out what his future in-laws were like before popping the question. He and Sheila are still married but there is a lot of stress in the relationship because she is about to have a baby and the cavalry is once again closing in.

No, he could not have changed his mother-in-law or sisters-in-law by completing this exercise, but he would have had more insight into what he was marrying into by doing a little more due diligence on the front end.

We can't choose our family members, but we can choose our mates. Getting involved with someone who doesn't get along with your family or vice versa does not mean that the relationship has to end. It does mean that clear boundaries should be set once you realize that a family member or family situation could pose a potential problem in your relationship. Don't sit back and think the issue will get resolved on its own or that it will just go away. Most of the time, the situation only gets worse with time. If possible try to work through the situation but if that is not possible, set clear ground rules on how the conflict or potential conflict will be handled between the two of you.

If you find yourself in a situation where you feel that you must take sides, you must understand that you should take your wife's side. She is the person that you are planning to commit the rest of your life to and she is the person that you are planning to sleep beside and build a family with. I hope that means something to you. If it doesn't you may want to rethink this marriage thing.

What do you do if your lady is in the wrong? You need to speak with her, calmly explain the situation, why you think she is wrong and be able to come up with a solution to resolve the matter, otherwise you may have a bigger problem than the conflict at hand to deal with. Your ability to communicate with her is essential to the success of your relationship. This is not only being able to talk about common interests and sharing your experiences but being able to resolve conflict. There will come many points in your relationship when the two of you won't agree. Ignoring the situation is obviously the easiest but not the most effective.

Your ability to talk to her and listen to her when you all disagree is fundamental to effective communication. When disagreements arise, you should not confront her with the intention of "winning" the discussion, but you should seek to understand her position and for her to better understand you. Reaching this common ground is a "win" for both of you and allows the disagreement to operate as a conversation rather than an argument.

Remember: seek to understand and to be understood. Your ability to communicate and resolve conflict will help when dealing with outside influences better known as family and friends.

To Do:

Surprise her by suggesting that the two of you spend a weekend at her parent's house. You should also make time to pay a friendly visit to your family's house. During your visits, observe her relationship and interactions with family members.

Her relationship with her mother will tell you how she will treat her best friend. If her mom knows everything about your relationship (including which underwear you wore last night), chances are her best friend knows also. Although the sharing of this information may seem trivial now, it could be a telling sign of how involved other people will be in the relationship. When problems arise, and problems will arise no matter how perfect your relationship is now, you need to be sure that you are the person that she will turn to when trying to create a solution.

The more people that have information about the details of your relationship, the more opinions the two of you will have to deal with in your conflict resolution. You may not be able to stop her from sharing this information with friends or family members but again this is the time to set boundaries about how you will deal with their interference in your relationship. It also may be helpful to point out the potential dangers of this information sharing because she may not even realize the possible consequences of having too many cooks in the kitchen.

A possible reference for you would be the movie written by T.D. Jakes entitled "Not Easily Broken." The main characters are married. They have some problems to arise in their relationship, the wife's mother moves in with the couple and becomes overly involved in the decision making of the relationship. Eventually, the wife has to choose between her husband and her mother, and she unwisely chooses her mother's side. The wife does not realize the emotional baggage that her mother brought into the decision-making process which influenced her relationship with her husband. She was fortunate to be given a second shot at choosing between her husband and her mother. Not all relationships are so fortunate. Often the choosing of sides can create irreparable damage between the two of you as couple and between you and the family member.

There will be times when people will want to give you advice about your relationship and you should always listen because you never know when you might learn something. However, before you follow their advice, it should be closely scrutinized to see what their reference point is for giving such advice.

Her relationship with her father is very telling of her expectations of you. If her father was absent from her life, get as much information as possible on how this has affected her, especially if she says it has not. The relationships that we observe as children effect the relationships that we have as adults. Having an absent or abusive father will definitely shape her expectations of her husband, however, you don't know if the impact will be positive or negative. Some people have a tendency to repeat the mistakes of their past while others move in the opposite direction, attempting to make things as different as possible. If you don't take the time to get to know her feelings about the subject, its influence may not become evident until you are years into the marriage.

If he treated her like a princess, you had better be prepared to take over that role. Some women will say that they don't have these expectations, which may be true but at some point, she may begin to resent you if you are not able to keep her in a lifestyle that she has been accustomed to all of her life. Once she is married, it is unlikely that her father will continue to provide for her. If he does, you have a slew of other problems to deal with because it is unlikely that this supplemental support will come with no strings attached. The father and/or the daughter may come to resent your inability to be the provider in the relationship. If you find yourself in this situation, it is key that you either discuss your current financial situation with your mate and what you can and cannot provide relative to the lifestyle she is currently living or speak with her father about his role in your relationship. You want to be sure that everyone is clear that you are the head of your family and it is your intention to function as such.

The worst way to deal with the situation is to pretend that you have everything under control. This pretense can only last for a little while and she may resent feeling as though she were tricked into committing to an unstable situation. I've dated guys that wanted me to think that they could "take care of me." It was obvious to me that they did not have the financial resources to do so but they thought it was necessary to keep me. Their dishonesty ruined the relationship. If they had been honest with me, I would have been more willing to work with them and their financial situation.

Her relationship with her siblings, if she has any, will be telling of how close she will be to your children. A doting big sister will no doubt be a doting mother however, a spoiled baby sister may have trouble realizing the sacrifices that must be made once you begin a family. If she has trouble dealing with your siblings this may a sign of a jealous streak that may extend outside of immediate family members to friends and co-workers.

You should always be leery of anyone that does not want you to associate with anyone outside of the household. In the beginning, the signs may be small like wondering why you have to go here or there but as the relationship grows, it may become problematic. Each of you are adults and you should treat her as such, and she should treat you that way also. This means that although you are a couple, you two are also adults capable of making adult decisions. If you two do not trust each other, your relationship has a very weak foundation which is a recipe for disaster.

You must also be aware of how her family treats you. If they don't approve of your relationship now, there is a slim chance that once you propose they are going to become your new best friends. If there are any problems between you and her family, attempt to clear the air and make your intentions for a future with Mrs. Right known.

Don't go into this situation trying to be the perfect future son-in-law because you are also setting the expectation of how you will behave in future situations. Don't be afraid to ask questions about the family tree or inquire about childhood stories. You need to gather as much information as possible about the wagon you are planning to hitch your horse to – how heavy is this load going to be?

Additionally, when visiting your family, you should listen carefully to her assessments of your family members. Is she overly critical of everyone or does she make obvious attempts to get to know them? Does she have a civil relationship with your mother, or can the tension be cut with a butter knife? Don't be afraid to ask your family for their honest assessments. Whether they believe she is God's gift just to you or the spawn of Satan, should not determine whether you propose to this female. However, it should make you more aware of some of her character traits, positive or negative.

*Hint: Don't EVER share insights received from your family members with your potential mate. Sharing any negative commentary will only cause problems because it will be hard for her to forget what you have told her that they think of her. She will remember those comments at every family event and will be suspicious of every future conversation that you have with this family member.

Also, if someone in your family is not fond of your lady, make sure that is clear that you will not tolerate any disrespect toward her. Some people may believe that because you were open to hearing their opinion, they now have free reign to provide commentary at their discretion. This should never be tolerated. You should also be mindful of your criticism toward any of her family members. Respect is received when respect is given.

Decisions...

☐ Gold digger – she expects you to pay for everything, constantly brags to family and friends about material items and wants you to show her parents a good time. It's almost as embarrassing as it is expensive!

☐ Drama queen – everything is an argument; no decisions can be made without extreme levels of emotion. Wow! Can you imagine a lifetime of this level of drama? Will she be as dramatic when communicating with your children?

☐ THE ONE – thank God that she's normal, her family is far from perfect but she's cool, there is no unnecessary drama, and everyone had a good time.

Notes to self: _____

_____

_____

_____

_____

_____

_____

_____

_____

_____

_____

_____

_____

Two

Let's Get This

Party Started

This project is going to measure the level of stress that you will encounter during the planning of your wedding, holiday events and any other gathering involving more than the two of you.

This may also be the first time the two of you work on a project together. Yes, I said it - together. It is imperative that you participate, or attempt to participate, in the planning of this event. Don't try to put all of the weight on her shoulders. Show your strength as a man and willingness to contribute in the relationship by taking on some responsibility. Don't be afraid to tackle something you may not have ever done before.

I suggested this to Alan before he proposed to Shatia. At first, he was resistant but to shut me up he decided to go along with it. You see, I have been out shopping with Shatia and I know how she spends money. Alan, on the other hand, is not very observant and can't tell the difference between a Louis Vuitton and a Wal-Mart purse. I hope that you can see where this is going. If not, you really need to read this book – closely.

Shatia and Alan decided to host a Super Bowl Party. Alan's idea of the perfect Super Bowl Party involved beer, his big screen, and some wings. Shatia...her idea of a Super Bowl Party involved decorations, dressing up in jerseys, of course hot wings (catered with all of the trimmings) and a full bar with a bar tender.

Either party idea, in my opinion, was going to be fun but because of the drastic difference in style, budget and ambiance; Shatia or Alan would be unhappy unless they were able to come to a compromise. My money was on Shatia because Alan always gives her what she wants.

Surprisingly, when they sat down together and started planning the event, they worked out a budget and Shatia made some concessions. I was even more surprised that she didn't go behind his back and overspend to get her way. She told me that she wanted to make him happy and agreed with him that some of that money could be better spent on something else – like, a new Gucci wallet for her.

To Do:

Host a dinner party or small gathering of friends and/or family members – together. Don't just tell her that you want to do this. Sit down, set a budget, divide responsibilities, and work together to make your event a success.

Start with the budget because this will give you a good look at her ability to co-manage funds with you. When discussing the budget does she have a realistic view of how much this event should cost? Is she able to stick to the budget or does she overspend? You may find that one of you is stronger with handling the finances than the other or that you are equally capable. This may help you to decide who and how you will manage paying household expenses once your union is official. You will need to make decisions such as will you pay for items from a joint account or will you divide the financial responsibilities?

Next is her ability to handle responsibility. Does she do what she is supposed to do, or does she expect you to pick up her slack? Does she trust you to handle your responsibilities or does she nag you to death about holding up your end of the deal? I didn't believe it but there are some guys that can deal with a nagging woman because things just roll off their back but there are some guys that insist on having the last word. It is imperative that you learn which guy you are and which female she is so that you can establish effective communication methods to deal with disagreements.

I've been told that if a man just agrees with his wife they will have a long and successful marriage. I find that hard to believe because in a partnership, you should each have a voice and neither voice should be louder than the other. I was once in a relationship and kept telling myself that an issue we were having didn't matter to me and I would just ignore it. Guess what? It and the relationship stopped mattering. Our thoughts manifest into our reality. If you continue to tell yourself that something doesn't matter, eventually it won't matter.

Finally, at the event, do you find yourself beaming with pride or so aggravated that you can't enjoy yourself? Beaming with pride obviously is the preferable emotion because you want to know that you can work together on projects as well as to realize each other's strengths and possibly identify some weaknesses in each other that you may be able to complement.

You can pretend not to see the signs but there will be more events – large and small and the patterns will be the same. It is imperative that you discuss your feelings about how the event progressed. Not many people are comfortable discussing feelings, let alone telling someone about your perception of their shortcomings. However, it is to your advantage to go ahead with the discussion and be open and honest about your observations. This is a two-way street because you were working together so be open to hearing her assessment of how the event played out from her perspective. Even if you do not agree, it can open some constructive dialogue that may eliminate or minimize future issues.

Decisions...

☐ Gold digger – does she expect you to pay for everything and spend like there is no tomorrow? Does she stick to the budget or splurge on the things she wants with no regard for your wallet?

Keep in mind that weddings can cost tens of thousands of dollars and not all brides' parents pick up the tab. Are you projecting a lifestyle to friends and family that is not consistent with your checkbook? If you are, forget the marriage counselor and start looking for a debt counselor. You may be able to afford it now but if the two of you are frontin' for your friends - you are on a fast track to accruing a mountain of debt.

☐ Drama queen – is every decision a problem? Do you have trouble agreeing on simple decisions like beverages? Does this little party make you want to throw this book away and wish you had never tried this experiment? If that's your reaction, you need to evaluate your strengths and weaknesses as well as hers. The drama may be the result of an increase in stress because neither of you have a clue as to what is going on or it could be that you are dealing with a confrontational person that will not be happy in any situation. Living in a constant state of stress will take years off your life. Talk to her about the disagreements and see if it is possible to find a resolution without causing more turmoil.

☐ THE ONE – you two work flawlessly together, the event comes off without a hitch (maybe a few hick ups but nothing either of you can't handle), you find yourself beaming with pride over your accomplishment. Enjoy sharing the spotlight with her and imagine how great it is to have a partner that shares your vision. With her by your side, you can accomplish anything.

Notes to self: _____

_____

_____

_____

_____

_____

_____

_____

_____

_____

_____

_____

_____

_____

Three

Not Tonight...

This may be the toughest project of them all, but it is the most necessary if you want a successful marriage. Everyone knows that when you get married the sex is not going to last at the same level as when you first started dating so you need to know if the brains are as good as the booty.

Fifty years from now, you want to know that you chose someone that you can actually hold a conversation with and share a peaceful retirement.

I shudder to think of my grandparents still getting their groove on but when they were alive, I loved to watch them operate as a unit. After so many years of being together, they knew each other's strengths and weaknesses and had so many stories of trials and triumphs to share. This bond did not develop from them spending most of their time in the bedroom together.

Couples today have become so sexualized that it seems as if they cannot operate without physical contact. Many guys don't understand what the waiting period is all about. Let me explain it. It is not our attempt at torturing you, but it is an attempt to test your seriousness about having a relationship. If you are not willing to wait a few dates, a few weeks, or a month to have sex, are you really trying to build a relationship?

Most women enjoy sex as much as men but if we had sex with every man that wanted our goodies, most of us would be able to make a living doing it. I am sure this is not what you want from the woman that you want to marry. In fact, you should appreciate it if your future Mrs. has strict guidelines about how soon she is willing to give it up. If she is loose with you... However, if she made you work for it, then you know that she is looking for something deeper.

Once you begin a physical relationship, it changes everything. The relationship is no longer about getting to know each other, especially if you have great physical chemistry. You are now looking at her through the lens of how much you enjoy being intimate with her. Believe it or not, I know guys that make exceptions for certain behaviors from women if they are good in bed. They are more likely to let a few things slide or let her believe the relationship is more serious so that they can continue playing in her sandbox.

For the sake of building a strong relationship, don't be so quick to get physically involved. Women are usually more turned on by men that aren't trying to get at them every five minutes. We like to know that you are interested but we also want you to give us enough room to make a move toward you. We decided when we first met whether you were going to get it, your actions going forward determine whether we change our mind. More men talk themselves out of the panties than into them. Focus on building a foundation and everything else will fall into place.

If your relationship is built primarily on sexual attraction, imagine what will happen if she is in an accident. Could you imagine yourself loving and caring for this person if she were no longer physically attractive or able to entice you in the bedroom?

Jahlil and Virginia have been married for eighteen; yes, count them, eighteen years. Jahlil does not take their relationship very seriously. It drives me crazy because Virginia seems really nice and he has admitted that it disturbs him that she isn't more of a free spirit. However, he says that she is a tiger in the bedroom, which is what keeps him going home to her every night.

He is an entrepreneur and has a large social network because of his business interactions. She has a standard 9-5 and a smaller circle of friends. He often comments about her being a slave to her job and not understanding why he works such odd hours and is always attending events with exciting people. He says that he hates to hear her complain about her job because she should just quit and do something that she really enjoys. Her constantly being stuck in a rut is becoming a drain on their *relationship because he can feel things starting to take off for his business.*

Jahlil admits that he thought she was everything that he ever wanted in a wife but...

There lies my problem. It is in the "but..." No one person will be a 100% match. When you start to focus on the "but..." in the relationship, you are allowing yourself to be excused from whatever action may come next as if it is somehow the other person's fault for not being your end all and be all.

She's everything I thought I wanted in a wife, but she doesn't have an entrepreneurial spirit, so I am going to hang out with Lisa because she understands.

My amateur diagnosis is that when we are in relationships that are not completely fulfilling, we go outside of the relationship seeking someone to fill the void. Because Jahlil and Virginia have two kids, two cars, college tuition on the horizon and a mortgage, he says that it is cheaper to keep her. WOW!

That is by no means the kind of relationship I would ever wish for anyone, but it is a possibility if you don't take the time to get to the person you are proposing to. In this case, it does not seem that they are communicating about their goals and finding common ground for the future. The things that they have in common – good sex, children, and a mortgage – are not the things that hold a marriage together. Marriage is legally binding which means you can't just walk away. Once you add children and promissory notes attached to joint collateral (houses and cars), you make it even more difficult to separate and have to rely on those things to justify staying with someone that you don't feel compatible with. Unlike a boyfriend/girlfriend relationship where you can just pack up and walk away when things get rough, you now have to get a lawyer involved and begin a process of detangling assets and sharing custody of little people who won't understand why mommy and daddy can't just make it work.

Before you make this level of commitment, decide to love her "because of…" and not "in spite of…" Don't reach the point where you have to overlook certain aspects of her personality to find your love rather try to find a way to love the good and bad because they all make up the wonderful woman in your life.

I once dated a guy and we were thinking about taking the next step and making it official. One day I asked him, "what do we have in common?" His response, "we both like to go out to eat and we like to watch movies." That immediately sent up a flaming red flag because if those were the only criteria for a lasting union, either of us could be with one of a billion people on this earth. I was amazed that he had not taken our relationship any more serious than our love for food and movies, yet he really believed this might be enough to sustain our relationship for eternity. I was mortified.

Sometimes I look around when I am out in public and see couples together, but they look miserable together. They look as if they wish they could be teleported to any place but where they are. Then I look around and see couples that can't stop talking to one another or touching one another. I am willing to bet that the couples that are not communicating are not doing so because they really don't have much in common or they haven't figured out how to communicate.

Do you really have anything in common besides good sex? Let's find out.

To Do:

If you are the one who usually initiates sex (which nine times out of ten, you are), then don't - for a week. (Note: this may be a good time to head to your local pharmacy to stock up on some lubricant). When you start to think about having sex, start talking about something you heard on the news, read in a magazine or in the newspaper or ask her some questions about her past, her today or her goals for the future.

I've heard guys say that they can't wait for sex or don't see the point in abstaining within a relationship. Sex complicates emotions. Men like to believe that only women tie emotion to sex but men do too. Men just do it in a different way. A woman sometimes believes that when a man is intimate with her it is because he has feelings for her. She may begin to imagine a relationship existing between the two of you and assume that you are obligated to her. Men, on the other hand, will have a tendency to put up with more things from a woman that he is having sex with versus one that he isn't. It isn't always because he loves her so much but because he enjoys the intimacy or sex that they share. Because he doesn't want the good times to end, he may listen to her nag a little more, make concessions that he ordinarily wouldn't make and even stick around a little longer in the relationship than he knows that he should. These actions are tied his emotions about the sex, but they are feeding into the emotions that the woman has about the relationship. She believes he is doing these things because he cares for her.

The exercise will help you to see her for who she really is and not just a package of goodies. It may not be easy, but it will be worth the sacrifice because if she is the ONE, you will be even more in love with her when you learn more about who she is and what she thinks about.

Although men can be very simplistic, women are eternally complicated. What we say is not always what we mean. We know that men rarely pry beneath the surface, so it makes it easy to keep things to ourselves and not involve you. By reaching her core, you will strengthen your relationship.

I watched a reality television show and this couple had been married for 20 plus years. The woman had an issue with hoarding, and it was getting out of control. The husband and kids were disgusted and could not understand why she could not let go of all of the junk. Once a therapist was brought into the situation to explore the root of the situation, there were details about her childhood revealed that caused an "ah-hah" moment for the husband and children. They could see why she was behaving the way she was. The therapist turned to the husband and asked if he knew about this childhood issue to which he replied, "no." They had been married all of these years, probably going to bed, and awakening together more times than not yet this very important detail which was creating a major rift in their family had never been revealed.

Don't be afraid if you don't like what you see. She may have some secrets in her past that she has been hoping to share with you but never found the time. You may be in a similar situation. Having the opportunity to put it all on the table is a worthwhile venture. Keeping secrets from one another is a recipe for disaster. Neither of you should enter into a union without fully knowing what baggage you are taking on or having the opportunity to share without fear of judgment.

I can admit that I am the queen of not sharing my feelings. So, if you ask if everything is ok, I may say yes, and chances are that you will let it go. What I really want is for you to sense that there is something wrong and pry for more information. Yes, this is very contrary to the nature of man but if you want to be with someone for the rest of your life, you need to be able to tell when something is wrong – before it blows up in your face.

Warning: execute this with caution. Make sure you have time to listen to whatever she has to say because women love to talk so once she opens up; it may be difficult for her to shut up. Score some bonus points by making sure the television is turned off.

You also need to practice "active listening" which is hearing the words that come out of her mouth, processing them in your brain and providing a response, even if it's just an affirmation like, "I know what you mean" or "Really, tell me more." Don't just say the words while replays of last night's game are going through your mind but really focus yourself on wanting to hear more.

To take this exercise to another level, start the conversation with "honey, there are some things that I would like to share with you." Share is the key word because you are encouraging her to be involved in the conversation. Think of something about yourself that she doesn't know but you think it is important for her to know. She may not know all of the questions to ask to find out the important stuff about you, but this will give the two of you a chance to build on what is already, hopefully, a strong foundation.

If you don't see her on a daily basis, you should attempt to not have sex during five consecutive encounters.

Decisions...

☐ Gold digger - If she's just with you for the money, she will be relieved not to have you pawing all over her. If this sexual hiatus does not bother her, you should be worried. She may not seem very interested in the conversation and may tune you out when you want to talk about yourself. Anyone not interested in knowing who you are as a person may not be the one you want to commit your life to.

☐ Drama queen – she's probably snooping through your things thinking you're cheating on her and I would not be surprised that instead of insightful conversations into each other's lives, you have probably been arguing about who you must sleeping with since she's not getting it.

If your attempts at reassuring her about your fidelity are rebuffed, then she may have some trust issues that the two of you need to work through. If there is no trust, you have no relationship. No matter how good everything else is in the relationship, you must be able to trust each other. You should also be aware if she is unwilling or unable to communicate when asked about her life. The drama may be a mask for other issues that she is dealing with. Encourage her to open up to you and let her guard down.

This personality type also isn't very interested in anyone or anything outside of themselves so you should not be surprised if your attempt to enlighten her about "you" becomes a conversation about her.

☐ THE ONE - she will be curious about why you are no longer seemingly turned on by her but she will appreciate your interest into her as a person, this will definitely bring you closer and you may be tempted to go out a buy the ring right away but hold tight, there's a little more work to do.

Notes to self: _____

_____

_____

_____

_____

_____

_____

_____

_____

_____

_____

_____

_____

_____

Four

Queen for a Day

Finding The ONE is an exercise in sacrifice. Today may be the ultimate sacrifice but the crystal ball into your future will become so much clearer.

You can learn a lot about your woman by figuring out how she spends her time. I may get in trouble with some of the women for this one but think of it like this: does your girl shop with a list or does she wonder from store to store? Does she get her hair and nails done on a schedule or just whenever? Are there certain stores that she frequents, or does she shop wherever is closest?

It is imperative that you know the answers to these questions because if your gut ever tells you something is going on (in a bad way), it will be difficult for you to find out the truth without coming across as a jackass. Knowing the answers to these questions will help you if you ever need to do a little investigating. By knowing her patterns, you will be able to tell when something isn't quite right.

I once dated a guy that said he wanted to know everything about me. It was a little annoying initially because I had never had a guy to take so much interest in me, but he spoiled me. After this relationship, I realized that I could not settle for anything less in my future relationships.

I realized that having someone take an interest in what makes me happy means that they are wanting to make me happy. I began to reflect back on previous relationships and realized that the guys didn't take the time to spend with me because they weren't that interested in me, as a person. You cannot imagine what a difficult revelation that was to come to, but it helped me to figure out what's important in THE ONE.

One of my guy friends, Kevin, told me that he would just randomly show up at his wife's job to take her to lunch at her favorite lunch spot. I thought this was so sweet until he revealed that he would do as a way to check up on her. Kevin scores bonus points with Jenn and her friends as the nicest husband for being so considerate but he also has a chance to observe her normal patterns and who from the office she is hanging around with.

Although I was a little miffed at him being so sneaky, I realized that it was a good idea. He says it keeps him from getting jealous of any of her coworkers and he likes seeing the smile on her face. She never knows when he is going to show up, so I imagine it helps to keep her on her toes a little bit.

Jealous can be an insane emotion but it can also be healthy. If you don't care about what she does, who she hangs around with or what happens in her daily life; you don't really care about her. Sad statement but true.

You can tell when a relationship starts to get serious because you will find yourself wondering what she is doing most of the time. You will want to know where she is at random times during the day. You will be concerned about that girlfriend that's single and drinks too much Tequila. Brace yourself – you will want to spend more time with her than with your friends.

Caution: jealousy is only healthy when it is kept in perspective. If you find yourself thinking of committing crimes, you have crossed the line from healthy to time to seek therapy or just walk away.

To Do:

Dedicate 24 hours to doing whatever she wants to do. I know that it may seem like a lot, but you will learn a lot so be observant. Not only will you learn what she likes to do and how she spends her time (years of gift giving ideas) but you will also start to piece together patterns. Knowing how she spends her time and who she spends it with can be invaluable information.

Be careful not to impose your wants and desires onto her day – remember it's all about her!

Try going into this thinking positive and genuinely wanting to spend time with the woman of your dreams. Yes, this is about investigating but don't forget to live in the moment and enjoy the time that you will get to spend with each other. You may also get some good writing material for your vows.

Decisions...

☐ Gold digger – everything you do today will be about you spending money – on her. You will probably accompany her to get her hair done, her nails done, to get a new outfit, out dinner, etc. You may enjoy walking around with an open wallet. It's your decision but don't look at this as a onetime occurrence. This is her opportunity to show you her world, what she enjoys and how much it costs. Pay attention!

☐ Drama queen – you can't wait until the day is over. It feels like the longest day of your life and you realize you like her a lot more in two-hour intervals. Twelve consecutive hours is more than any human should be required to spend with her.

You've argued about everything from clothes to driving to what you're going to eat. The makeup sex may be great, but you never want to do this again.

I highly recommend that you discuss your feelings with her and try to assess why you had problems getting along.

☐ THE ONE – today helped you to see how much the two of you have in common. Hanging out with her was like hanging out with your best friend – in fact, she is your best friend. Today wasn't bad, it was nice. A lifetime of this won't be bad; you are looking forward to it.

Notes to self: _____

_____

_____

_____

_____

_____

_____

_____

_____

_____

_____

_____

_____

Five

Step Back

If you are considering proposing, the two of you have probably been on a few dates and may have a few spots that you frequent. More than likely, these hot spots are all within a certain price range. This exercise is going to shake that up and see how well she adapts to change.

The only constant in life is change. You will be faced with change at every turn and you need to know how she will deal with that. The ability to roll with whatever life deals you is essential to living a happy life individually as well as together.

Have you ever met someone that constantly complains whenever something doesn't go his or her way? You know the person; they are never happy unless they are the center of the universe.

Almost every woman wants to be the center of her husband's world. She wants to believe that he will do everything in his power to take care of her and to make her happy. To marry him, she wants to know that he will forever have her best interest at heart.

The only problem... you are human. At some point, you may not be able to be all of those things. Something may change. Your relationship may reach a state where things are no longer as they were when the relationship began. What happens next?

My boy, Jesse, started dating a girl that was out of his league. After meeting her for the first time, it was obvious to everyone. She was decked out in designer labels from head to toe and they were not knock offs. Jesse could only afford to take her out once per week because he would have to wait until payday so that he could afford to wine and dine her at the trendy nightspots.

We all told him that he should just 'fess up. If she really liked him, it wouldn't matter how much money he had. She would understand.

Jesse wasn't trying to hear that. He kept playing this charade and was about to finance a ring that he would have probably never been able to pay off. We wouldn't let up. We were like, "Jesse you have to come clean."

Well, one week his paycheck was short because he had to take some unplanned time off earlier in the week. So, he goes to pick up Anne Marie and takes her to a chain restaurant rather than the trendy spots where all of her friends hang out. We were shocked when Jesse told us that she was cool about it.

However, she never returned his calls after that. Something else could have happened on that date but I doubt it. Jesse was upset but says that in hindsight he wished he had done that earlier to find out her true intentions. I was just happy he didn't finance a small planet and get himself in a lot deeper.

To Do:

Plan a date night but instead of going to one of your regular dinner spots, take the date down a notch. If you normally drop a bill on dinner, budget for $50 instead. If you normally go formal, try casual.

You can even mix it up, get dressed up and head to McDonald's. This isn't about the money but you need to know that if you lost your job or were downsized, she could take that step back with you and have the confidence in you that one day she will be eating high on the hog again.

To increase your chances of success, keep your focus on her and don't make a big deal out of the change. Just say that you feel like something different tonight. If you make a big deal out of it, she probably will too.

This project is short and sweet, but it will open your eyes about her true motivations in the relationship.

Decisions...

☐ Gold digger - she is going to be very confused and very unhappy. She is accustomed to a certain level of dating and will be appalled that you think so little of her. The higher her gold digger quotient, the more you should downsize. If you are afraid of losing her over this stunt, then you never really had her. To sustain a successful marriage, you need someone who is going to be by your side through the ups and downs.

☐ Drama queen - any time you go against giving her exactly what she wants, you are igniting her fuse. The test is how much drama one meal will cost you. Imagine if this downsizing were necessary for three months. Could you handle this drama for three months?

☐ THE ONE - she may be a little confused, but she just enjoys spending time with you. She may even express her displeasure but explain that this is what you have a taste for, and I am sure she will be willing to accommodate your desires.

Notes to self: _____

_____

_____

_____

_____

_____

_____

_____

_____

_____

_____

_____

Six

Hit the Road

Traveling as a couple is a huge commitment because you have to rely on each other for efficiency and entertainment. If one of you is running late then you will both be late. Sitting in an airport, riding in a car, guess who is going to be your primary source for conversation?

When traveling somewhere where neither of you know anyone else, you become the only source of companionship for each other. If this proves unsatisfactory and you start looking outside of the relationship for companionship, already... you might as well signal Houston because you have a problem.

In order to make this successful, you have to plan a trip to a location where neither of you know anyone except each other.

My girlfriend, Suzanne, was deeply in love with Drew. However, they argue about everything. They will argue about how bright the sun is shining when it's raining outside. It drives everyone nuts especially when we all go out to eat because we can all predict that they will have at least six arguments about absolutely nothing in the course of a two-hour dinner.

I suggested that they take a trip because the day-to-day stresses may have been what was causing the tension in their relationship.

One day Drew announced that he was taking Suzanne away for the weekend on a ski trip. I was intrigued. I could not imagine what was going to happen when the two of them were left alone. Would the arguing escalate, or would they find harmony?

Upon return, Suzanne announced that she and Drew broke up. I was somewhat surprised and a bit relieved. Obviously, I had to ask why, and she explained that even though opposites sometimes attract they realized that they were better as friends than as a couple. She said that while they were away they had a chance to really talk and get to know one another and realized that they argued so much because they didn't have very much in common, even though the sex was good, and they enjoyed hanging out with each other.

To Do:

Take a trip together – just the two of you. You can surprise her, or you can plan it together. You can go away for a week, a weekend or overnight. The key is to get out of both of your comfort zones and see how well you interact. It doesn't have to be elaborate but once again, it will provide some relationship clarity.

Sometimes we are so caught up in the day-to-day operations of life that we miss many of the little details. It will be helpful to take a step back from your normal routine and get to know each other in a neutral environment. Take the time to really listen to what she really likes to do. Does she prefer being active like skiing or rollerblading or would she rather sit by a fireplace and watch the snowfall? You have a lifetime of family vacations ahead and it is important to know what each of you enjoys.

Don't preplan everything rather decide together what you will do when you arrive. Use this time to evaluate your ability to make decisions together and reach compromises. A friend once told me that marriage is all about sacrifice and communication. At each stage in the game, you both must be willing to make sacrifices in order to reach compromises and you have to be able to communicate your willingness in a spirit of love.

Hint, hint – there's a honeymoon on the horizon. Don't you want some way to gauge how much fun you're likely to have before you make the commitment?

Bonus: if you are feeling extremely brave, make the commitment to turn off all electronic devices and distracters. That means no cell phones, MP3, radios, televisions, etc. How long can you make it only being able to communicate with each other? I shudder to imagine a day without my BlackBerry, so I know that when I find a man who I am willing to disconnect from the world for... I have found the ONE.

Decisions...

☐ Gold digger - she will be focused on where you're going, having the best accommodations, and being pampered. You may have the same travel style but make sure that this is an area that you agree upon. After all, who wants to fight every time you plan a family vacation?

☐ Drama queen - it doesn't matter what you do, you two will be arguing about something at some point in your trip. Ask yourself if this is how you want to spend every vacation for the rest of your life.

☐ THE ONE - she will appreciate being able to spend some time alone with you. Take this opportunity to continue learning about each other. This may be the beginning of a cosmic star alliance.

Notes to self: _____

_____

_____

_____

_____

_____

_____

_____

_____

_____

_____

_____

_____

Seven

Bling, Bling

You may find this easy or you may have some serious reservations. It doesn't matter. This is essential. This will in no way reflect your feelings of worth about her, but she may not see it that way. This will reveal how much she appreciates you and your efforts to make her happy. It may cost a little, but it could save you a lot.

The old adage, diamonds are a girl's best friend, is true. I (personally) don't know of any woman that will turn down a diamond. Diamonds may not be every woman's favorite because there are tons of beautiful stones in an array of colors on the market. I do not doubt that lovers of other gemstones exist, I just don't know any. Your girl may be this anomaly but if you present her with a diamond, I doubt very seriously that she will make you take it back.

However, this is about something much smaller than a diamond. Outside of diamonds, women can be very particular about jewelry. Some women only want to wear gold while others wear platinum or silver and some load up on costume (fake) jewelry.

The options are limitless and your observations of her taste in jewelry speak volumes about how well you know her. Close your eyes and imagine her favorite piece of jewelry. If you cannot do so, you may need to spend a few days observing her and what she likes to wear.

One night I received a phone call from Courtney. She sounded concerned so I asked what was up. She said that Rod had just come home and brought her a gold necklace with a "C" charm on it. I was confused. What was the problem? She said, "He must be up to something. He never just buys me jewelry like this."

I tried to explain that maybe he was just doing something nice. She would not hear of it. On top of all of that, she explained that she never wears gold and could not believe that he didn't know that.

I felt sorry for both of them. Sorry, that Courtney could not appreciate Rod trying to be spontaneous and do something nice and sorry that Rod didn't know enough about Courtney to know that she doesn't wear gold.

A situation that could have been extremely romantic and endearing became a wedge in their relationship because she obviously didn't trust him, and he didn't know her very well.

Prior to that, Rod had confided that he thought Courtney was the ONE. This situation opened his eyes and he began to see some other personality issues that helped him to realize that they were not as compatible as he once thought. He said that he wanted someone who could appreciate him and his small love offerings.

To Do:

Buy her a piece of jewelry – just because, no holiday, no special occasion. Aim for a bracelet, earrings, or a necklace - nothing extravagant. Don't try to make it into something special. Give it to her as a 'just because' gift.

If you have a hard time picking out something that you think she will like then you really don't know her very well. If you are prepared to marry her, you should know a great deal about her – including her taste in jewelry.

To avoid finding yourself in Rod's position, it may be helpful to observe her jewelry collection for a couple of days. If you see chunky pieces, it may not be a good idea to go with something fragile whereas if she wears lots of different colors, just ask her favorite color as a good starting point.

This will also provide insight into her ability to appreciate the two months' salary (yes, two months is customary) that you will be spending on her engagement ring. Look at this like a trial purchase.

Decisions...

☐ Gold digger - her eyes will instantly begin to appraise the value of your gift. She won't hesitate to let you know whether you did a good job. Just beware that she may begin to expect more 'just because' gifts.

Yes, your feelings should be hurt if she wants to exchange it for something else or return it and get the money. This is about the thought and her ability to appreciate your efforts.

☐ Drama queen - she will find something wrong with gift even if deep down she really loves it. Her ability to find satisfaction in the small things in life could be a sign of her inability to find happiness in life period. You might want to reflect on her ability to be happy in general. Is this a rare mood for her or is she always displeased with something?

☐ THE ONE – she will be sincerely impressed with your efforts and will treasure your gift. She will probably want to wear it immediately and may not take it off for several days. The look on her face may even be your incentive to give her more 'just because' gifts.

You want to know that no matter how small or how great your offering is, it will be appreciated.

Notes to self: _____

_____

_____

_____

_____

_____

_____

_____

_____

_____

_____

_____

_____

Eight

Dream House

We all have dreams of the future and when we get married some of those dreams must mesh into one common future vision. You may be living your dream while she isn't or vice versa but to have a successful marriage; you must be working toward a common goal.

Buying a home is probably one of the largest purchases that you will make as a couple. It may also be one of the biggest compromises that one of you will ever make.

Remember, creating a solid foundation for your relationship is all about sacrifice, compromise, and communication. These factors will be essential when deciding where you want to live and what type of home. This decision may not seem important right now but imagine you envisioning living in a downtown condo while he dreams of having a large backyard for weekend bar-be-ques. What if you are thinking

of spare rooms for poker night and she's
planning a nursery?

I knew that my friend Jason was head over heels in love with Annette. However, Jason lived in a one-bedroom apartment with bare furnishings and did not see the importance in spending money on drapery, wall hangings or dishes. Annette's apartment, on the other hand, was color coordinated to the coasters. I wondered if Jason had considered how much Annette was willing to spend to decorate her lovely apartment.

Knowing how much Annette likes new homes and interior decorating, I suggested that she and Jason take the local Tour of Homes one Saturday morning. Jason was not feeling it, at all. However, we convinced him that it would be fun.

Following the tour, Jason called me and was freaked out. He thought they were going to look at some moderately priced homes, but Annette was looking at the million dollar plus homes. I asked Jason if he talked about this with Annette and naturally, he responded that he had not. I advised that he hang up and immediately call Annette to express his concerns.

Needless to say, doing so helped to clear the air. Annette explained that of course, those were her dream homes, but she knew that it would be virtually impossible for them to ever afford one of them.

I am happy to report that Jason and Annette have been married three years and bought their first (moderately priced) home two years ago.

To Do:

Take a Saturday or Sunday and go looking at houses. Let her show you her dream house and listen to her decorating ideas and visions for the home. You will learn a lot about what she likes and her goals for the future. You can take that information and look at what she's doing today to get to that point – or does she see you as her meal ticket.

Although every man should want to provide for his family, that is a huge responsibility. If you make $40,000 a year and she's looking at million-dollar mansions then there may be a disconnect – unless she makes a substantial amount more than you or there's a plan to get you all to that level.

If you feel uncomfortable with the houses she's looking at, talk to her about it. She may realize that these homes are out of your range but enjoy the fantasy. This can be dangerous because you will have to live with knowing that you may never be able to give her what she really wants.

I met another couple that had just gotten married. We were looking at the wedding pictures and I began to ask where they were planning to live. Sunita began to describe the doublewide that her parents lived in and how much she would like one just like it, out in the country, one day. I could see a look of utter confusion on Kristopher's face because they obviously had not discussed this detail. It took all that I had not to burst out laughing but I often wonder if they ever discussed the issue before or after this encounter.

This is just one of the ten signs but to some this may be one of the most important. If you allow someone the freedom to dream, you will learn of their innermost desires.

Decisions...

☐ Gold digger – she probably already has her dream house picked out or at least the neighborhood that she can see herself living in. She knows exactly how she wants it furnished and it's not going to be cheap. Can you afford it? Will you be able to afford it in the future? If not, you guys need to talk because this isn't just a dream for her, this is the expectation of the future and she won't settle – for long.

☐ Drama queen – what may start out as a fun adventure will surely turn into an argument. The two of you obviously have something in common or you would not be considering creating a lifelong union with her, but you need to be sure that it is worth it.

On the other hand, this may be an area where the two of you can come together and bond. Look for commonalities in your dreams and use that as a foundation for your future.

☐ THE ONE – the two of you are probably on the same page about a lot of things and this exercise will provide one more opportunity for you to learn more about each other. Don't be afraid if she has grandiose dreams because if she is the ONE she will work to get you all where she wants to be and won't hesitate to incorporate your dreams into her master plan.

Notes to self: _____

_____

_____

_____

_____

_____

_____

_____

_____

_____

_____

_____

_____

Nine

I Forgot My Wallet

This one could get you into some trouble because those are four words that most women don't want to hear her date utter – unless she really is the ONE.

Most women, no matter how independent they want to be, want a man to take care of them. I would like to believe that most men aspire to be a provider and take care of their woman. I have never been a proponent of going dutch on dates or even volunteering to pay on a date. Call me a gold digger, whatever. I just believe that women should be courted, and part of courting is paying for dates.

However, I would never ask more of a man than I am willing to give. Hearing my date say, "I forgot my wallet" is not really my greatest fear but definitely, something I plan for before each date.

The idea for this came when Troy and Carla went out and Troy, accidentally, forgot his wallet. He didn't think it was a big deal until he told Carla and he said that she flipped out. He was shocked. He thought about all of the meals that he had paid for without expecting anything in return and then about the one meal that she had a problem loaning him the money to pay for.

Fortunately, they realized that he had forgotten his wallet when they tried to order drinks, so he was able to keep the bill to a minimum, but he told me that the meal wasn't the same and neither was their relationship after that incident.

I can imagine the hurt that Troy must have felt but as with all of these projects, I believe that it is better to see people's true colors sooner than later.

I once went out on a date with a guy that had been stressing me about going out with him for weeks. Once I finally gave him a chance, he said that I had to come and pick him up because his roommate had his car. I was cool because stuff happens. But when we got to the restaurant and he said, "You got me, right?" I almost fell out of my seat. This was our first date and he was already on this level, not even let's go dutch but looking for me to be the provider. A man has to understand that when a woman is asked to be the provider, she expects to have to power and privileges that come along with this position. Those are the same powers and privileges that can emasculate a man in a relationship so don't start this mission too soon or use it too often.

I hear so many men complain about women being too independent in relationships however they don't make any attempts to show her that it's okay to relax and allow him to take control.

Most women in our society have not had the luxury of women from previous generations. In the past, women were wed in their teens or early 20s and did not have to learn to take care of themselves or to operate as the single head of the household.

In recent years, more and more women have had to take on this role and some of them grew up in households with a single parent and no example of how a successful relationship operates. If this was her situation, it may necessary to spend some discussing the role of the man and the woman in the relationship. Although this conversation may seem elementary, it is imperative that each of you understand your role in relation to the other.

One major difference between relationships of the past and today's relationships is that more and more couples are seeking partnerships.

Although the male hopes to operate as the head of the household, many women want to have a voice in the relationship. To sustain a successful marriage, you must clearly identify your expectations of each other. However, a partnership implies that you have her back as much as she has your back. This type of security will be a cornerstone in the foundation of your marriage and building trust in one another.

To Do:

On a date night – not during your Step Back date night, a girl can only handle so many surprises – at one of your regular spots, wait until the check comes and tell her that you forgot your wallet. If you normally pay for dinner, this will come as a huge shock. If you normally split your meals, which would be odd, she may not be as surprised, but you will want to see her reaction to paying the full tab. If you take turns, make sure you do this on your night to pay.

This exercise will tell you quite a bit about her financial stability and whether she can afford the lifestyle that the two of you are living.

By the way – even if you leave your wallet at home, make sure you bring your ID and some money or a credit card. I don't want to see you in jail or looking like a fool if she can't pay for the meal. If she does pay, offer to pay her back, and make sure you follow through as soon as possible. It will solidify your trust in her as well as her trust in you.

Decisions...

☐ Gold digger – she is not going to be happy and may exhibit some drama queen behavior. If she does pay for the meal, she may be angry at you for being irresponsible and putting her on the spot whether she has the money or not.

If she doesn't pay, then you may be in a situation where she is trying to come up through your wallet. Not necessarily a bad thing but definitely something you should be aware of.

☐ Drama queen – be prepared for her to create a scene. There is always a chance that she will surprise you but more likely than not she is going to read you your rights – maybe at the scene of the crime, maybe when you get home. Again, imagine you lose your job and are forced to rely on her income for some period of time. Will she have the same reaction every time she is required to whip out her wallet?

☐ THE ONE – you have no qualms about this exercise because you know she has your back. I hear the fireworks display setting up.

Notes to self: _____

_____

_____

_____

_____

_____

_____

_____

_____

_____

_____

_____

_____

Ten

The Book Store

There are thousands of books in a bookstore. Whether she loves to read or only reads every other page, there is a book in the bookstore that is perfect for her.

Imagine yourself walking to a Barnes and Noble or Books a Million, surrounded by books. You think about your honey. You imagine her sitting, peacefully, reading a book. The only question is which one of the thousands of books in this store would she enjoy reading?

If you have really applied yourself to any of these projects, this one should be a breeze. The two of you have planned an event together, you have traveled together, you spent a week talking, not having sex (didn't you?) and you've seen her idea of her dream home. You can pick any one of these interests and find a book for her. If you are still having trouble, then I suggest you do some serious thinking about whether you are ready to get engaged.

I will make this story personal. A guy that I was dating, let's call him Eric, decided to buy me a book. I was so excited because no one had ever bought me a book and I really enjoy reading. However, this book was so boring, and I read about five pages and started wondering what in the hell made him buy this book for me? What was he thinking? Who did he think I was? The signs had been there that we were not compatible, but this was bigger than a red flag, it was a red rocket aimed directly at my relationship. Needless to say, we are no longer together.

To Do:

Go to the nearest bookstore and buy her a book. This is similar to the Bling, Bling but it may surprise you more than her. Browse through the different sections of the store and think about her. Think about what she likes to do, where she works, what she wants from life and buy the book that you believe she would most like to read.

The point of all of these projects is not to point out her flaws or to highlight your differences but to allow both of you to go into your marriage with open eyes. It is imperative that you know the person that you say you want to spend the rest of your life with.

Decisions...

☐ Gold digger - it will be surprising if she appreciates your gift because it has no monetary value, unless you buy her a book about money, which is a telling sign into her true personality. Be prepared for the book to go unread but process this along with the other nine signs and see what you come up with for your future.

☐ Drama queen – this may be an area for you to score some points. I can't image why someone would become angry over a book but it's possible. If your girl becomes angry about a book then you have a serious problem – that you are about to commit to for the rest of your life. By this point in your missions, the two of you should be much closer and she should be opening up to you.

If you are still hitting your head on the same brick wall, she is not likely to change.

☐ THE ONE – she will appreciate your token of affection and will be touched by the sincerity of your gift. This exercise will have brought the two of you one more step closer and should give you the confidence that you are entering into a union with someone that you know and trust.

Notes to self: _____

_____

_____

_____

_____

_____

_____

_____

_____

_____

_____

_____

Who Am I Marrying?

	Gold Digger	Drama Queen	The ONE
Family First	☐	☐	☐
Let's Get This Party Started	☐	☐	☐
Not Tonight	☐	☐	☐
Queen for a Day	☐	☐	☐
Step Back	☐	☐	☐
Take a Trip	☐	☐	☐
Bling, Bling	☐	☐	☐
Dream House	☐	☐	☐
I Forgot My Wallet	☐	☐	☐
The Book Store	☐	☐	☐

MY GIRL IS _____

Gold Digger

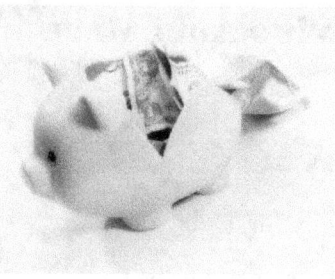

If you have assessed that your girl is a gold digger – and you still want to marry her – then I applaud you. You must be mentally strong, emotionally secure, and financially stable. She is prone to tantrums and will expect the best of everything. She will not accept disappointment and wants you to be on your A game at all times. She will always look good on your arm and will create an atmosphere that many will envy.

Be aware that there may be a lack of substance behind the extravagance. As you build your family, your financial responsibilities will increase. Make sure you have a financial plan and stick with it. Although you may enjoy indulging Mrs. Right, don't do so at the detriment of your financial stability. Make sure you have a nest egg tucked away for hard times that will allow you to continue living your lifestyle until things get better. In your case, this nest egg should be about one year of your monthly outflow – including bills, shopping, salon visits, etc.

On a deeper level, there are many women that want the stuff, but the stuff is a mask for an emotional void that is missing in her life. In many instances, their true feelings are hidden behind a perfect façade that no one has ever been able to penetrate. Most of the women that I know keep themselves together physically to keep from falling apart emotionally. It is my hope that although she may come across as all about the money, these exercises have helped to reveal some endearing qualities about the gem within.

Women are treasures. Sometimes the true value is evident from the moment you meet, sometimes it takes a strong man to penetrate the tough exterior and find the diamond in the rough.

You should not enter into a union that is based solely on your ability or desire to give her stuff because you will never be able to give her enough stuff if you don't take the time to get to know the woman within. Not only will she be unable to find satisfaction in the relationship, but it could also result in some problems on your end because you may one day seek a deeper connection that she is unwilling or unable to provide. Realizing this upfront will help you choose to be in this situation rather than feeling like you have been deceived.

Drama Queen

Your Mrs. Right is a drama queen – and you still want to marry her? I wish you the best of luck. Don't go into this union thinking that one day she is going to change. It's not impossible but don't hold your breath because it is not likely. There is obviously something going on with her that is causing an extreme amount of unhappiness and she brings that baggage into every situation.

You may be a glutton for punishment and enjoy the constant unrest but consider how this behavior will affect any children that you may have. Kids thrive on stability and need to be in nurturing environments. You may want to consider holding off on the proposal and working to establish a stronger bond that reduces some of the chaos in your relationship. This is not only for your benefit but also for the sake of the family that you may be interested in starting.

Otherwise, commit yourself to working through the multiple obstacles that will present themselves. If you know who she is when you propose, you are not allowed to become fed up or angry with her for continuing to be who she is a few years down the road. Go into this with your eyes wide open, in love with this woman and willing to support her and her insanity.

The ONE

She's
The ONE
and I
couldn't
be
happier
for you.

It is obvious that the two of you communicate very well and have lots in common. You will inevitably have your ups and downs in this relationship, but you would rather work through your problems than live without her.

All relationships require work and at some point, you will experience temptations outside of this union. When you find yourself in this situation, ask yourself if you are willing to throw everything away for what may amount to nothing more than a fling.

Past generations were able to withstand the test of time because no matter what problems they faced, they faced them together. They were willing to work through their problems and not give up when times got tough. It is for that reason that 25 years later when they were too old and too tired to do anything but hold hands or sit and look at each other; their bond had been strengthened not only by the good times they shared but by the tough times they endured.

If she is The ONE, commit to making every day better than the last.

The Man in the Mirror

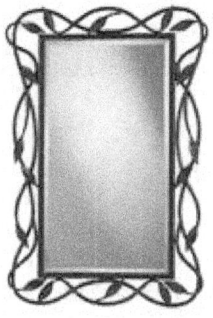

Obviously, we have done a lot work on figuring out who your girl is and where she is coming from but it's time to look at the man in the mirror.

What are **you** really looking for? This lady, this queen, this precious person is assuming that when you present her with this ring, you are ready to make a lifelong commitment to her. She believes with all of her heart that you are the man of her dreams ready to stand by her until the end of her life. Is this what you want?

Being in a relationship is a very different level of commitment than a marriage. In a relationship when things start to go sour, you have an easy out. Even if you live together, you just pack up and leave. If you have an argument, you go to your boy's house and chill out.

A marriage, on the other hand, means that you stick it out. You enjoy the good times and you work through the bad times. You have to communicate. You can't say that it doesn't matter. You can't look to the hot, single, no-strings attached woman that shows up at the most convenient times.

No, you have to go to the source and talk. Most guys don't like to talk but women do and until both sides have their positions heard and a compromise is reached, the problem is going to get swept under the rug.

First, let's deal with what happens when you don't compromise. I know guys are taught to fight until the death but if you go into a disagreement knowing that you are going to have to give a little and you are going to get a little; your strategy will be much more effective. Women for the most part want to be heard. We want you to understand where we are coming from, regardless of how long it takes us to communicate it and regardless of how crazy it may sound to you. Communication, open and honest, is the key to making a relationship work.

Next, you may think sweeping a problem under the rug is ideal because it is tucked neatly away, and you don't have to deal with it. She's not talking about it and neither are you. This may seem like a great set up, but it is slowly killing your relationship. Remember how I told you about my relationship and me saying that I didn't care. It is amazing how your self-talk can change your way of thinking. Imagine some habit that your girl has that really annoys you. When you propose to her, you are saying, "I accept you just as you are." You are accepting all of the good stuff as well as all of her crazy.

Have you ever heard a couple about to separate say that they just grew apart? They grew apart because they were not growing together. They were not using those disagreements to make their relationship stronger. They were not looking for a compromise. Each person was looking for a win. But, in the end, everyone loses with that strategy. The more problems that are swept under the rug, the greater this mound becomes, and it eventually separates them.

Building a successful marriage is a lot like building a house. You won't agree on everything like the color of the drapes or your favorite restaurant, but it is these little differences that give your home and your relationship character. These are the differences that you see in each other and help you to enjoy the act of compromise.

But there are certain parts of building a house and a relationship where there should be no compromise. This is your foundation. When creating a foundation, you want it to be solid, sturdy, and sure. You don't want to guess whether it will ever fail you or if it can be penetrated. We all know what the foundation of a home entails but not many of us realize that the foundation of a successful relationship requires us to first analyze what is most important to us in terms of education, family relations, handling finances and disagreements, social status, etc. Yet we bring other people into our lives, for what is supposed to be a lifetime, and not only don't we know what matters most to us, but we don't know what matters most to them.

These projects were designed to focus on building a strong foundation for your future marriage. I hear so many guys talk about "taking care of a woman" or "being the man" in the relationship but how many of you have looked in the mirror and thought about what this means.

Taking care of a woman is about more than satisfying her in the bedroom or with your wallet. It is also about taking care of her emotions and her heart. We are a product of our life's experiences. Not all of those experiences were positive and many of them have caused us, men, and women, to take on relationship habits that are not conducive to a healthy long-term relationship.

Take a moment to look at the man in the mirror and be sure that you are ready for the level of commitment that is symbolized by your proposal.

Time to Pop the Question

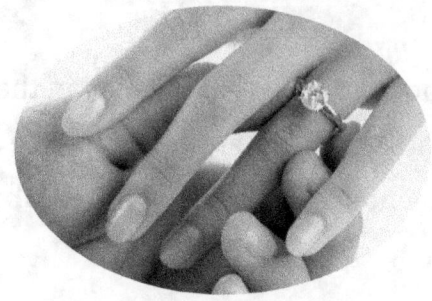

If you have completed each of the missions in this book, then we've been together for a little while. In that time, I hope you have learned a great deal about the woman you hope to share your life with as well as a few things about yourself. The labels gold digger and drama queen are not meant to be nasty or to inspire negative feelings about your mate, but I hope that you will take away a realistic notion of the person that you are planning to wed.

Some male personalities are more suited for a gold digger than a woman perceived as THE ONE while a drama queen is not necessarily compatible with a man attracted to a gold digger. It is not likely that your mate will fit into one category for all ten projects, but she will fit into one for the majority and you will see some telling signs into your future.

It is just as important to determine what you see in her as what she sees in you. Will she appreciate you for who you are today and not who she hopes that you will one day become? Can she accept the gifts, the trips, and the lifestyle that you can provide her or is she looking for more and pushing you to be someone that you are not?

I wish you the best of luck with your proposal and many, many years of unimaginable bliss.

About the author...

LaKesha Womack is a first-time author inspired by the men in her life to write this book.

She says that witnessing so many men and women go into engagements and subsequent marriages with glazed eyes prompted her to write this book and hopefully it will create a greater awareness of the person they intend to spend the rest of their life with.

Womack admits that she doesn't have any formal relationship training, however she states, "I have many guy friends that make the decision to get married but when I ask them simple things about the woman in their life, they don't have a clue. In the beginning the relationship is a novelty and sometimes after being with someone for so many years, marriage just seems like the right thing to do."

"However, I grew up with my grandparents as relationship role models and they seemed to have a connection beyond the superficial and they committed to staying together through the thick and the thin. That is the type of commitment that I hope each person who reads this book can achieve."